BERTA L.

Discovering
The Quantocks

SHIRE PUBLICATIONS LTD

Contents

Photography by Douglas Allen

Copyright © 1974, 1977 and 1980 by Berta Lawrence. No. 195 in the 'Discovering' series. ISBN 0 85263 660 1. First published 1974; second edition 1977; third edition 1980; fourth edition 1984.

Introduction

Over these wild and beautiful hills at all hours of day
and night, in all seasons, have I wandered and never
in vain. (Andrew Crosse)

The Quantock region gives the impression of space, solitude and
wildness, in spite of its limited area. The range is only twelve miles
long, with a ridgeway along its spine, and is nowhere so broad that
some distant village cannot be glimpsed. The south-west side
dominates the fertile Vale of Taunton, the misty Brendon Hills
and blue distant Exmoor; the north-east looks on part of
Sedgemoor, farms, the coast, the frowning towers of Hinkley Point
nuclear power station, the Bristol Channel with the islands of
Steep Holm and Flat Holm and, in clear weather, the Welsh coast.
At St Audries (West Quantoxhead) the Quantocks roll down to the
sea. Villages, apart from Broomfield and Bagborough, shelter at
their foot.

The hills undulate softly; Will's Neck, 1,260 feet, is the highest.
The summits make a heathery moorland broken by gorse thickets,
whortleberry-bushes and seas of bracken and are treeless except
for hollies, gnarled hawthorns and an occasional pine. Here sheep
and ponies find rough grazing. Slopes, particularly on the
seaward side, are grooved by deep and lovely combes, some
wooded, some conifer-planted, and watered by streams, their sides
smothered in bracken, ferns, foxgloves or rhododendrons. The
combes shelter ponies and sheep and red deer hide in the bracken
where in autumn the russet-bronze colouring blends with their
own. Fox and badger also find a home, as does the adder. Red
tracks go through the combes and over the hill-tops. Smaller paths
and little green sheep-tracks meander down side-slopes. Barrows,
the burial mounds of prehistoric men, lie concealed by the
heather; two or three hills are crowned by Iron Age camps. In
several places pools serve as deer-ponds; the slot of the deer is
plainly printed in their surrounding mud, as at Wilmot's Pool near
the old Green Path that runs from Dead Woman's Ditch to
Halsway Post. The most desultory walker can find his way,
especially if he carries a map.

The following are some of the hills, starting from the Coach
Road (i.e. the Crowcombe Road off A39).

Past Dowsborough (or Danesborough) on the right, the road
wanders over Great Bear. At the top, on Robin Upright bear left
and pass Black Hill, Hare Knap, Black Ball, Hurley Beacon,
Crowcombe Park, Crowcombe Fire Beacon, ending at Bagborough
Hill and Will's Neck. Longstone Hill, Stowberrow Hill, West Hill
can be reached from Holford via Dog Pound Lane close to the
gates and old Dog Pound of Alfoxton.

The principal combes and hills are named on the Ordnance Survey map. All of them are beautiful although in places the conifer plantations have removed hard-wood trees, wild flowers and much bird-life. New plantings of beeches are a welcome sight. Cockercombe, Ramscombe, Seven Wells Combe, Quantock Combe, Weacombe, Bicknoller Combe, Butterfly Combe, Hodder's Combe and many others are a source of delight in all seasons, as Andrew Crosse said. Most of this region has been designated an Area of Outstanding Natural Beauty. It will remain so if it is cherished by all who use it.

Great care should be taken about fire hazards and depositing litter. The playing of transistor radios spoils the peace of the hills for others.

There are good facilities for riding holidays in the Quantocks, and there are youth hostels at Crowcombe and Holford. Most of the villages have good guest-houses and inns.

The Somerset Trust for Nature Conservation at Fyne Court offers special courses on Quantock studies.

It is hoped that lovers of the Quantock Hills will become members of the Friends of Quantock, an association founded for conservation and enjoyment of the area. Apply: Hon Treasurer, Mrs M. E. Bryant, The Mount, Courtway, near Bridgwater, Somerset.

The new Quantock Society, based at Holford, is actively concerned with special Quantock problems.

1. Durleigh

Durleigh is the first village on the hill-road from Bridgwater to Taunton. The manor-house called West Bower looks across Durleigh Reservoir which covers its former orchards. A severe drought lowers the water so that the lines of their old paths are revealed. Two semi-octagonal towers (1500) guard the arch of a vanished gateway. One has a stone staircase. Their upper floors contain very pretty little rooms that recently lost the original ancient stained glass from their two-light windows. Most regrettably, the circular dove-cote with conical thatched roof, a well known local landmark, has collapsed into non-existence. This little manor is the reputed birthplace of Jane Seymour, third wife of Henry VIII.

The reservoir, which supplies the British Cellophane factory and a large part of Bridgwater, is fed by the swiftly tumbling stream called Durleigh Brook that rises in Holwell Combe in the Quantocks. This sheet of water is the delight of local ornithologists as it attracts birds in their hundreds: herons, cormorants, grebe, snipe, wild duck, an occasional kingfisher, swans, and the noisy gulls from the river Parrett and sea-shores. Not all these birds are popular with anglers, nor with the Reservoir Warden who lives at the old Durleigh Mill opposite the church and supervises the hatcheries for the eggs of brown trout. The little fish are transferred to stewponds and finally to the reservoir where they grow delectably plump.

The small red church with its fourteenth-century saddle-backed tower faces the mill. (It has lost its dedication.) Part of this church has stood here since Norman times. The prehistoric Quantock trackway runs out from behind it, whitened in places by wild garlic that some say is proof of the Romans' footsteps.

Rexworthy Farm has the remains of a moat.

2. Enmore

Spring bowers this village in red-flowering chestnuts and red hawthorns. At all times the red note predominates; ploughed fields are red; castle, cottages, barns are built of red Quantock sandstone. Their background is green parkland, pastures, hedgerow trees, belts of woodland, and forestry plantations like Wind Down on Enmore Hill.

The pseudo-baronial Enmore Castle is the remains of an imposing eighteenth-century 'Gothick' building with Victorian additions. It retains the old underground stables. In 1807

Coleridge, staying at Nether Stowey, came here to visit John Perceval, Earl of Egmont, who greatly admired his genius. The Percevals' castle replaced a medieval castle owned for generations by the Malet family. The funerary helmets of two Malets hang near the chancel arch in the church where one member of the family served as priest. These were found during demolition work at the castle. The Early English church (St Michael) has a Norman doorway with zigzag decoration, an Early English west door and a black oak Jacobean pulpit richly carved.

Opposite the church stands Castle Farm. The attractive house is L-shaped and has the Dutch gables popular in the mid seventeenth century and windows surmounted by a semi-circular arch and keystone. The adjacent long grey cottage is the old Poor House transformed.

The Rev. John Poole (cousin of Coleridge's friend Tom Poole) who built the former rectory, now Poole House, in a garden near the main road also built Enmore village school in 1810. The six sandstone cottages in the main street were built for their rents to .support it. It was the first free primary school in England, attracted much interest and still functions admirably.

The road to Spaxton runs through Barford Park, close to Barford House and its walled garden. A fine red-brick eighteenth-century house flanked by pavilions, it was triumphantly rescued from near-ruin (plate 1).

The prehistoric Quantock trackway can be made out running alongside the main road through the village.

The sign of the pretty old inn, the Tynte Arms, is painted with the armorial bearings of the Tynte family who for many years were seated at Halswell House, Goathurst.

3. Goathurst

An extremely pretty little village, still far from the madding crowd, Goathurst may be reached from Broomfield, Enmore or from North Petherton on the A38. The winding lanes offer views of peaceful, pastoral landscape over their hedges. A stream babbles down the village street that is bordered by cottages of appealing charm; cream, white, yellow, pink or sandstone-red, some with dormer windows, their mossy tiled roofs all shades of red, brown, green. Lyre Cottage has a lyre design in the ironwork of its porch.

The changes in village life are proclaimed by several of these houses: The Forge is a pretty building made from the former blacksmith's premises—his chestnut-tree has gone but nails and horse-shoes turn up in the soil; the Old School House was the village school; the red almshouses of 1780 make two attractive houses; the Old Rectory (now two houses) was once a manor-house; while the houses round the courtyard of Halswell House, the former seat of the Tynte family whose last representative was Lord Wharton, were at one time the butler's house, the orangery etc.

The great park of this house creates a certain melancholy. Part is ploughed, part used for grazing and some fine trees remain. But the wealth of magnificent timber, admired by such writers as Arthur Young, has been removed since the Second World War—oaks, beeches and giant Spanish chestnuts whose disappearance has exposed the charming rotunda and little temples dedicated to the Druids, Robin Hood and Love. Decay threatens them. Sir Halswell Tynte built the mansion in 1689 to replace an older one.

The church bears the unusual dedication to St Edward; a painting of his martyrdom by Richard Ansdell, a Goathurst artist, hangs in the church, a Perpendicular building with tower of earlier date, built of a deep-red sandstone. It holds multiple memories of departed Tyntes and their ancestors, the Halswells. Their hatchments splash colour on the tower walls. An elaborate monument with urn and weeping woman adorns the nave. In the north chapel there is a most elaborate tomb-chest with sculptured effigies of Sir Nicholas Halswell and his wife surrounded by nine children as 'weepers'. On the south side there is the Halswell chapel with frieze of painted shields, and a set of funerary armour, including helm and fourteenth-century sword. A strikingly lovely tomb in the walled churchyard, for John Willis and his wife, dated 1702, is sculptured with *putti* and garlands. It supports a Corinthian pillar bearing an urn and carved, as Collinson described, 'with emblematical designs'.

4. Cannington

This is a large and growing village of great interest. Its associations deserve a detailed study.

The high red sandstone church-tower with its gilded weathercock dominates miles of countryside. The impressive church (St Mary) has many of the oldest and prettiest cottages, as well as the old Globe Inn, grouped near it in Church Street. Its other neighbour is Cannington Priory, now used by Cannington College which also possesses other premises and a farm. The mullioned windows of this beautiful sandstone house—Elizabethan with later alterations—look on to a courtyard. A low fragmentary wall represents the original Benedictine priory of 1138 where according to legend Fair Rosamond de Clifford was brought up. A thirteenth-century ring engraved with the de Clifford arms and now in the British Museum was certainly found in this village. The Rogers family was prominent here. In 1672 Henry Rogers left money for restoring the derelict church house (used for village ale feasts). Its use as an almshouse has survived as in 1971-2 it was reconstructed to form five dwellings. From 1672 Cliffords occupied the court-house on the Priory site. In 1807 another Lord Clifford settled Belgian Benedictine nuns there. Some of their graves lie behind the high walls on the Bridgwater side.

Brymore School at the other end of the village is a Technical Agricultural School. The great Parliamentarian John Pym was born in a house on this site.

Appropriately, in this village that is a centre for agricultural activity, the vicar blesses a plough at the church door on Plough Sunday and at Rogation-tide leads a procession of children carrying spring flowers on staves to bless the fields and the brook. The choir stands on the bridge beyond the main bridge (there is a little pack bridge too) and sings.

Blackmore Farm is a house of ancient beauty; it retains its domestic chapel. Several fine Georgian houses also adorn the main street, notably the house at its junction with the Hinkley Point road.

The latter road which leads seawards reaches Cannington limestone quarry and an expanse of uncultivated humpy ground called Cannington Park.

This ground has mistakenly been called the site of the Battle of Cynwit and is marked Cynwit Castle on the Ordnance map. Bones visible in the quarry-side were thought to be those of Danish warriors until expert excavations revealed hundreds of skeletons interred in an early Christian burial-ground (fifth to seventh centuries). The Saxon warpath (*herepath*) winds away from this locality to cross the Quantocks.

The interior of the truly majestic church is almost daunting because of the great height and austerity of its walls. In recent years it has acquired beautiful specimens of modern artists' work: an altar frontal, a crucifixion mosaic, a crucifix in the baptistry, sculptured figures of saints for the niches in the west front. John Pym is said to have presented a chalice in 1633.

5. Spaxton

This far-reaching parish takes in several hamlets — Radlet, Merridge, Pightley, Splatt. The Saxon names are interesting: *Splatt*, a strip of land; *pightle*, a little plot. The name Splatt is attached to the fine old mill near the church, the last of several to stop working here. There was a bakery at the same place. Its great ovens and ceiling-beam made from a tree trunk remain in the sturdy old house. Two derelict cottages five hundred years old in a forsaken orchard made the beautiful house called Splatts, with a trout stream in its garden, that is Splatt Mill's neighbour.

At Pightley a house called Peacock Cottage, because of its yew-tree's shape, contains decorative seventeenth-century plasterwork.

Spaxton is a place of ancient farms that include Tuxwell near Radlet Common (now cultivated). This property belonged to several generations of Blakes, the great admiral's relatives, and down to modern times possessed a Blake's Orchard. The farm called Currypool had a mill mentioned in Domesday Book. Currypool is the name of the stream that flows on to feed Ashford Reservoir (*Curry*, peculiar to Somerset, Devon and Cornwall, may represent a Celtic name for a stream). Another of the streams audible in Spaxton is swift-running Peart Water, *peart* being a Chaucerian word for brisk or sprightly. The imposing Old Rectory is now called Peart Hall.

The L-shaped manor-house now called Court Farm stands near the church. Both are built of red sandstone silvered by lichens. Here is another millwheel formerly worked by the rushing stream and now mossy with disuse. This is a beautiful corner of the old village.

A red-tinged path approaches the church (St Margaret) passing venerable yews, tombstones grey and green with age and the canopied fourteenth-century cross. A modern sculpture of St Margaret stands over the porch.

Here is another Quantock church interior deserving much more detailed description than can be given here. A Geometric east window and a window-splay in the north wall indicate an early date for the north aisle. The Perpendicular south aisle has a waggon-roof with gilded bosses. In the chancel the very fine effigies of an unnamed knight and his lady (c. 1460), who were perhaps Hills of Spaxton, lie beneath an elaborate canopy. Probably they were sculptured in a Wells workshop. The crowned angel carved in oak near a pillar has a Flemish look. The sixteenth-century bench-ends are boldly carved with such motifs as plants and heads inside medallions. One of them, called the Fuller's Panel, is famous; it illustrates a clothworker with a length of cloth and the tools of his trade. 'Fuller' is a misnomer, as he is clipping or 'finishing' the cloth. Spaxton once had an inn called the Clothworkers' Arms.

A human touch is given by the names and farm-names cut on pews by restless boys in 1728: 'Ed West for Stevens' (a farm);

9

'John Thomas for Crockers', etc. A rugged old almsbox made in the seventeenth century with three heavy iron locks is still in use.

There is a memorial to Sir Robert Crosse of Charlinch who died here in 1602 — 'knighted for exploits at sea and for laudable services to God, Prince and Countrie, especially against the Spanish Armada'. A slab in the chancel floor commemorates Joseph Cooke, a rector, who in 1708 left land to provide 'an hospital and 2/-p.w. to 6 poor persons and 4/-p.w. for an honest man to read morning and evening prayers to them'. The back of Cooke's Almshouse is seen from the churchyard, a long stone building that has been modernised to continue its kindly work. It still possesses the old prayer room.

In the nineteenth century the most commented-on buildings in Spaxton were those of the Agapemone at Four Forks, now turned into private houses. Here the Rev. H. J. Prince of Charlinch established his community who regarded him, and his successor, as the Messiah. The creation of it caused scandal, but in recent times the Agapemone housed a quiet law-abiding community.

6. Charlinch

This, too, is an out-of-the-world village that appears deceptively small because its farms are scattered among fields reached by long shady lanes. The core of the village is splendidly sited. The high churchyard, where the spring grass is splashed by snowdrops and violets, looks southward over meadows and cornfields towards distant villages and church-towers. Near its yew-trees a kissing gate leads into fields. From the field-gate opposite the church gate another colourful Quantock landscape sweeps for miles; it includes fields with a 'terraced' appearance.

The church has a Norman south door and nave. The font too is Norman with a seventeenth-century dunce-cap cover of carved oak. Most of the building dates from the fourteenth century except the little fifteenth-century south transept that is graced by an east window, on the glass of which four female saints are portrayed against a blue background: St Sitha or Petronilla, with keys and book, St Catherine, with sword and book, St Apollonia, with tooth in pincers, and St Cecilia with hand-organ.

Wall tablets commemorate members of the Blake family, some of whom lived at Padnoller, the L-shaped white house near the turn to Fiddington (A39). A brass in the chancel commemorates Jasper Bourne of Gothelney Hall. The reading-desk was made from the wood of Tom Poole's oak.

In this church filled with the murmur of trees the Rev. Henry James Prince, curate, frenziedly proclaimed to a credulous congregation that he was a modern incarnation of the Messiah. He founded the religious community at Spaxton called the Agapemone or abode of love.

The enormous old rectory in the red-walled garden full of trees that include a veteran fig-tree has been divided into a spacious Georgian house and The Tudor House that is Elizabethan. Here is an outstanding example of the huge rectories built, with coach-house and stables, to accommodate large families with numerous servants drawn from the village.

Gothelney Lane rambles to Gothelney Green a mile east of the village, and here Gothelney Hall, built about 1500, hides itself away. Its past owners include the Hodys (including a Lord Chief Justice) and the Bournes. A Bourne of Gothelney was one of Blake's officers and fought against van Tromp, the great Dutch admiral.

The banqueting hall of this manor-house was divided into two storeys in the seventeenth century so that the remains of the minstrels' gallery and the fifteenth-century ceiling are in the upper part. The mullioned window of the hall, looking on the forecourt, has only a little left of the heraldic glass retained until the Second World War when the house stood unoccupied or used for farm stores. Left of the two-storeyed porch stands a sandstone tower pierced with loop-holes. The Hodys built it in 1460. At the top there is a small chapel with angel-corbels on its roof.

Robert Crosse, fellow-seaman of Drake and Raleigh and knighted by Queen Elizabeth I, came from Charlinch.

---

7. Aisholt

'A deep romantic chasm . . . down a green hill' was Coleridge's description of the hidden valley in which Aisholt lies, when he wanted to live there (plate 3). Even today the village gives the impression of being miles from anywhere — which was Mrs Coleridge's objection to it. This peaceful remoteness, however, in conjunction with the beauty of the surrounding countryside, endeared Aisholt to the poet Sir Henry Newbolt who in the 1930s spent much of his time at the Old School House which is the thatched cottage with a thatched porch sheltered below the steeply placed church. The latticed window of his writing-room looks on the garden and the lily pool where he watched the kingfishers. Since his time the house has undergone some extension and alteration.

Aisholt has a number of thatched cottages, some on the crest of the slope, some down in the hollow, as well as sturdy old barns and

11

farmhouses bearing ancient names like Bishpool (Piscis Fontem), Chafflock and Durborough.

Going to church entails an uphill walk as the church is very steeply perched, looking down on the combe and beyond it to some of the reddest Quantock ploughed fields, groups of trees and slopes covered with heather and ferns. This is one of the most endearing small churches (All Saints) that recent renovation has skilfully rescued from a rather forlorn state. Except for the Perpendicular top of the tower, it is early fourteenth-century work. The interior appeals by reason of its simplicity and intimacy: white walls, a thick inner wall pierced by a huge squint, the painted arms of Crosse over the south door, a chancel arch of red sandstone, a parish chest made from an oak-trunk. In the nave floor the tomb-slabs of two Blakes, father and son, each called Humphrey, record the deaths in 1663 and 1664 of close relatives of Admiral Blake.

Aisholt got its name from the ash-trees of the Quantock forest where the Saxons settled. The red deer still shelter under the beeches and ashes of Aisholt Wood and a stream runs under the trees of the Aisholt valley. On the way to Spaxton the new reservoir on Hawkridge Common (enclosed into fields), which is fed by this stream and another, has not detracted from the charm of the area. Sometimes it is dotted with coloured sails of little boats. There is a sailing club.

In the evenings the reservoir often lies in solitude and water birds haunt it undisturbed.

8. Over Stowey

This little village lies well away from main roads in a high position under hill-slopes coloured by gorse, heather, bracken and particularly rich in whortleberries. In the 1890s the novelist Phyllis Bottome, whose father was rector, spent several childhood years in the old rectory opposite the church gates, and in her autobiography *Search for a Soul* she left a marvellous picture of the Victorian village, its inhabitants, its lovely scenery and its farms lying 'under steep red fields' endowed with old names like Strawberry Hill, Fuzz Ground and Cockley Land. In its layout this tranquil place has hardly changed. (There is another house called the Old Rectory on the other side of the church. It contains interesting plasterwork.)

The church (SS Peter and Paul, formerly St Mary Magdalene) has undergone considerable restoration. Its bench-ends have good Tudor carving. The glass of several windows came from William Morris's workshop and was designed by Burne-Jones. One depicts Mary Magdalene and the angel at the tomb.

The brass chandelier came from the Bridgwater brass-workers and bell-founders, Street and Pyke, whose handiwork, with that of their associate, Thomas Bayley, adorns a number of Somerset churches. Particularly appropriate to this rural area is the wall monument (1815) to two brothers, John and James Rich, who were wealthy farmers. It incorporates the plough and harrow, a beehive and rakes, as well as a sarcophagus. James Rich of Cross Farm presented the chandelier in 1775.

The village contains several hamlets. At Adscombe the big farmhouse of Adscombe Farm, its russet-brown barns and a group of old cottages stand near a gurgling stream that runs down from beautiful Seven Wells Combe. Scouts sometimes camp at Adscombe and there is an authorised camp-site called Great Wood Camp that has been popular with school parties. At Marsh-mills the very pleasant eighteenth-century house standing at the crossroads near the old mill was the home of the Rev. John Poole who very reluctantly received the youthful Coleridge and Southey here in 1794 when they first visited the Quantock district. From here the road to Aisholt turns left and runs through Plainsfield, another hamlet, where the late Quantock Weavers, at the Old Forge for nearly fifty years, made beautiful fabrics coloured with dyes made from Quantock plants—gorse, lichens, madder, sloe, whortleberry. This road passes Quantock Lodge — now a school — that was built by Henry Labouchere, later Lord Taunton, MP for Taunton (Disraeli was his opponent). The peculiar green stone was quarried on his estate, to which the Stanley family succeeded. William Morris's daughter, Jenny, spent her last years at Plains-field and was a friend of the weavers. She died here.

If you turn right, however, on leaving Over Stowey church, you will pass at a right-hand corner the Jacobean house of Cross Farm with its gazebo perched on the garden wall. This road leads to Bincombe, close to the hills and a favourite place for whortleberry-pickers. Some of the most beautiful combes as well as some of the most ancient roadways lie inside Over Stowey parish, for instance Seven Wells Combe with its springs and streams, and Cocker-combe near Quantock Lodge with its thickets of rhododendrons.

The Stowey Road — an ancient name — which climbs to Bincombe is part of the Saxon *herepath* or warpath.

9. Nether Stowey

Part of this village has been designated a 'conservation area' and justly so, for without being as beautiful as some of the Quantock villages it has a most interesting character and is rich in historical associations. In the eighteenth and early nineteenth centuries it was a market-town with a market-cross at the junction of Lime Street and Castle Street. One of its most arresting features is the noisy brook flowing from the Quantocks and along a deep brown-pebbled bed down Castle Street and along part of St Mary Street—'the dear Gutter of Stowey', Coleridge called it. There is a line of very old quaint cottages in Castle Street, and on the other side Poole House, a handsome Georgian dwelling spoilt by a large shop-window. Behind it stand the remains of outbuildings that served the tannery owned by Tom Poole; the bark-house where he dried oak-bark for tanning has recently become a house. Cottages now cover most of the tanyard and the garden with the lime-trees and arbour familiar to Coleridge whose Lime Street garden connected with Poole's. Tom Poole was friend and benefactor of the whole village and beloved by many men who became distinguished, as Wordsworth said. At this house Poole entertained Coleridge, the Wordsworths and Charles Lamb. In 1813 he gave land in adjacent Tanyard Lane to build the village school where it still functions. By 1805 he lived at The Old House (its present name) in St Mary Street where the Coleridges, de Quincey, Humphrey Davy and Southey visited him. When he died, his business partner Ward called his death 'a moral earthquake' for Nether Stowey.

Coleridge's cottage in Lime Street (plate 5) is cared for by the National Trust and is open from March to September, attracting many visitors. It had become the Coleridge Cottage Inn, before public effort rescued it, and retains the iron arm of the inn sign. It was tiny, thatched and uncomfortable when Coleridge lived there and wrote almost all his greatest poems including 'The Ancient Mariner' and 'Christabel'. The Wordsworths walked here frequently from Alfoxton and Charles Lamb came on a summer visit when Coleridge wrote 'This Lime Tree Bower'.

The Women's Friendly Society founded by Poole still exists and at midsummer walks in procession from the Rose and Crown to the church, every member carrying flowers. After the service the 'walk' ends at the Rose and Crown for tea — just as in 1806.

Any walk to church holds more perils since the busy bypass changed the original layout of Stowey and cut off the church, Stowey Court and Stowey Court Farm on the Bridgwater side. The church (St Mary) was rebuilt, except for its tower, in 1851. Before that it probably possessed a singers' gallery, to build which Edward Gibbs bequeathed £60 in 1640. Two mitres on the walls commemorate former vicars who became bishops. Tom Poole's memorial tablet mentions his close friendship with the poets. His inscribed tombslab lies outside near the south door.

The baptistry commemorates a greatly loved Stowey nurse and has oak woodwork made by a modern Stowey craftsman.

After the First World War the Somerset writer Walter Raymond lived in the attractive old house at Stowey Court Farm where he wrote some of the essays collected in *Under the Spreading Chestnut Tree*. Stowey Court has great charm, standing behind a sandstone garden-wall crowned by a yew hedge and an eighteenth-century gazebo. It was garrisoned during the Civil War when some of the church registers, housed there for safety, were burnt. Part of it was built in Elizabeth's reign, the work having been commenced and then relinquished when Lord Audley, its owner, was executed for supporting Perkin Warbeck's rebellion. Its stonework incorporates some stones from the Audleys' vanished Norman castle that until the Wars of the Roses dominated village and countryside from Castle Hill, the 'mount'. The keep foundations have been uncovered; its walls were six feet thick. Sheep graze now among the gorse-bushes on its site, which in its time has been used for bear-baiting and rough sports.

The village 'runs' hundreds of sheep on the Quantocks, and ponies too—an ancient right. The ponies are rounded up at Bridgwater Fair time.

The adventurous Elizabethan Jesuit Robert Parsons was born in Nether Stowey in 1546, supposedly the blacksmith's son. Many times he risked execution, frequenting London 'dressed in a suit of buff with gold lace and a hat with a feather'. He died in Rome in 1610.

---

10. Holford

Visitors come to Holford for two reasons: its scenery and its Wordsworth associations. The buildings on the A39 would not tempt them to turn up the lane past the old Plough Inn and site of the old smithy, both known to the Wordsworths, but a few yards' walk up the lane brings them to enchanting thatched cottages and to Holford Glen (part of Alfoxton grounds) where trees hang over the waterfall and the rushing stream flowing to Kilve. Here Wordsworth wrote 'Lines Written in Early Spring' and his sister Dorothy noted the oaks, hollies, periwinkles and ferns in her journal. Cottages have been built in part of the Glen since their time; the little silk-mill, now in ruins and unsafe to approach, was then in use. Bearing right, and round the Glen wall, one reaches the old Dog Pound and the gates of Alfoxton Park. (The older spelling is Alfoxden.) There is a right of way through it to Pardlestone Lane and Kilve, under fine old trees sheltering the thick holly wood Wordsworth knew.

Now a very attractive hotel, the charming eighteenth-century house—white with classical pediment, Tuscan porch, slate roof—has not greatly changed if one discounts the Georgian addition on the north, the loggia and the new swimming pool. It faces a slope which is a platform for the great oak the poets knew and where deer still move in the bracken at dusk. Just beyond is Longstone Hill and the brown Great Road under the famous Holford Beeches that stand half-bare and wildly contorted by sea-winds (plate 4).

Holford provides access to lovely Quantock places. Outside Alfoxton gates the Bowling Green path leads past the woods of Willoughby Cleeve (National Trust) to Hodder's Combe, shaded by beech and oak, watered by a stream. Alternatively the road's left-hand fork, near the Glen, runs past a line of thatched cottages to become a rough shady lane passing eighteenth-century Combe House (a hotel) and its water-wheel that once served a tannery, to Tannery Combe, also called Butterfly Combe, which holds a pool and is cut by a stream with stepping stones. Like Hodder's Combe this combe is damp enough to grow rushes and bog-loving flowers. From both combes little green paths radiate up wooded slopes, up to heathery hill-tops, down into other combes. Butterfly Combe lies in the shadow of Danesborough (Dowsborough) on the left as you enter from the lane. This hill, second highest in the range, is crowned by an Iron Age camp of ten acres, surrounded by a ditch full of scrub-oak and a double rampart overgrown with heather. It provides a long-range view of the sea.

The very plain and simple small church (St Mary) with gabled tower and saddleback roof is in keeping with the village, although much restored. It retains part of its ancient cross in the church-yard.

Frederick Norton, the composer of *Chu Chin Chow,* is buried here. Virginia and Leonard Woolf honeymooned at the Plough.

Beautiful Shervage Wood (National Trust) is in Holford parish and so is Woodlands Hill (National Trust) that looks towards eighteenth-century Woodlands House where John Kenyon, cousin of Elizabeth Barrett Browning, lived.

Memorials of the St Albyns who owned Alfoxton for many years and were Wordsworth's landlords are in Stringston church, close to Holford. The house was formerly in Stringston parish. There is a small St Albyn chapel in this endearing little church that has a red-tiled broach spire.

11. Kilve

Putsham, the main part of this village, connects with the grounds of Alfoxton House at Holford via hilly Pardlestone Lane where the little stream encourages primroses and ferns—a Words-worthian walk. On the right, near the Hood Arms, a mile-long lane runs past Kilve Mill, now disused, and follows a stream that has run under the road towards the church, Priory Farm, the priory ruins and the sea. The grey stone of these buildings is blue lias, quarried from the jagged crumbling cliffs that fall from the fields to a beach strewn with stones. Curled fossils, or ammonites, are embedded in the cliffs. Care must be taken when walking the field-path near the cliff edge — a pleasant pastime on a summer day when sea breezes stir fields of tall grass or ripening corn.

Smugglers used the creek called Kilve Pill during the Napoleonic Wars and hid their brandy-kegs in lime kilns, still visible in many coastal fields, as well as in the ruined 'Priory' which suffered much damage when the kegs were set on fire one night to defeat the excise officers. This building was never a priory but a chantry for five priests, founded in 1329 and disused before the Reformation except for agricultural purposes which it has long served. Now the roofless yellowish-grey walls roped with ivy are unsafe to enter (plate 6). A hollow in the field marks the Priory fishpond.

Priory Farm possesses a cattle-shed and barn of the old type that is now such a rarity: built of stone, roofed with red-brown tiles and supported by a line of stout circular stone pillars. The churchyard lies under a purple-brown hill and dark woods; it provides a view of the Court House at East Quantoxhead. Heavy stone tombs crumbling with age, lichen-stained, smothered in ivy, flank the path. The small austere grey church, restored in 1861, consists of nave and chancel and retains several ancient features. Outside one notices on the south side the Tudor priest's door and a projection like a small tower with a pretty medieval window set just above the pulpit. One chancel window contains fragments of golden medieval glass, one displaying a Lombardic M, the others leaf-sprays. The Norman font has cable-moulding. Part of the fifteenth-century oak screen, with tracery and vine-leaves, is in the belfry.

Photographs in the Hood Arms testify that not many years ago the sport of 'glatting' was practised along the shore at Kilve. At a season of very low tides men took buckets, sticks and terriers to discover and despatch conger-eels hiding in pools under boulders.

In 1914 the poet Edward Thomas stayed at the Hood Arms.

Kilve Court—an eighteenth-century house—is now a Residential Youth Centre. Some of the courses it offers involve walking in the Quantocks and along the coast with special study of their flora, fauna and geology.

Kilve Common is hill territory in the shadow of Danesborough (Dowsborough). Here is the source of a stream, a little spring called Lady's Fountain that must have been named before the Reformation.

12. East Quantoxhead

A unique village where time seems to have paused—at least with regard to the place, rather than to the life of its inhabitants. The Luttrell family have held it since 1230 and their Paganel ancestors from the Conquest onwards. Court House, church, mill, Court Farm, the village pond and clustering thatched cottages—here is the traditional layout of the English village, set between the crescent of the hills and the sea (plate 7).

The Court House is built of grey lias stone quarried from the coast—as is the church where huge fossils are embedded in the walls—and the lime for mortar came from kilns in the fields behind it, near the sea. The main portion is E-shaped; the battlemented west front and south front are dated 1500, but the more ancient parts are concealed, for example the Cock Court and primitive bakehouse with a floor of cobblestones. It possesses striking plasterwork overmantels embodying scenes such as Christ's entry into Jerusalem as well as swags of flowers and heraldic devices, made by Flemish plaster-workers employed at Dunster Castle in the early seventeenth century and whose names, Levercha and Lascarse, remain in West Somerset.

The house has a fascinating history. It is not open to the public.

The austere little church (St Mary), approached by a path bordered by turf and flowering shrubs, has a chancel with an arch of blue lias and a tower with a fourteenth-century arch of red sandstone. The Elizabethan pulpit has leaf-carving, and bench-ends are carved with a wealth of berries, leaves, thistles and the Luttrell device of six martlets. There is the sixteenth-century tomb, with sculptured canopy, of Sir Hugh Luttrell.

Looking out through the church porch one sees it as the frame for a landscape of hills, combes, woods and fields.

The circular thatched barn near the mill is called the Round House. Here a horse used to turn the mill for cider-making.

In 1784 a little limbless girl called Sarah Biffen was born to poor parents in one of two cottages that now make Townsend House at the corner of the lane close to the A39. Sold later to a fair-owner and exhibited as a freak at Bartholomew Fair, she attracted attention by her skill at sketching with a brush fixed to her shoulder, found a titled patron who paid for lessons and then became quite famous as the Armless Artist with a talent for portraiture. Royalty patronised her. She made an unlucky marriage, was granted a pension by William IV, won the Society of Arts medal in 1821 and knew poverty in later years. Her gravestone in St James's Cemetery, Liverpool, is inscribed:

Reader, pause.

Deposited beneath are the remains of Sarah Biffen.

She was born without legs or arms at East Quantoxhead County Somerset'.

In 1925 Liverpool Art Gallery held an exhibition of her miniatures.

13. St Audries or West Quantoxhead

Here at their western extremity the Quantocks curve down to the sea. From several viewing points (near the Quarry car-park for instance) the seascapes can be quite beautiful on days when the water takes on a pearly sheen, but seen closer it is often sullen-coloured. However the sea rolls in towards bright red cliffs streaked with grey, green and blue. A field-stream becomes a cascade that pours over a cliff-side, and at the top of one cliff there is a hollow place called the Grotto. (Warning notices point out that in places these cliffs are crumbling and dangerous to sit under.)

This is an interesting length of coast where the sea sometimes washes up whorled fossils and where mammoth tusks, now in the County Museum, Taunton, were found. The mammoth roved a prehistoric forest of which fossilised fragments sometimes show themselves at low tide.

The way to the sea is through the entrance of Rydon Lodge off the A39. A path twists between copses of fir and beech to drop between cliff-sides to rock-steps and the beach. Little frequented for half the year, the shingly beach is a popular place for summer picnics. St Audries Bay is sandy. St Audries Holiday Camp (chalets) has its entrance gates on the A39.

The village shelters under Stowberrow Hill, now dark with conifers. The church and a private road to the manor-house and home farm lie immediately beneath. The manor-house is now St Audries School for Girls. Both house and church were rebuilt in 1856 by Sir Peregrine Acland, who built the village school also. Tales are told of smugglers who lived in cottages, now demolished, behind the school.

The church is dedicated to St Etheldreda or Audrey, first Abbess of Ely in 679. The Doulting stone of its structure looks a little alien in this region of red sandstone, but the roof, with its corbel-angels bearing musical instruments or the signs of the

Passion on shields, is of Quantock oak; the blacksmith from the hamlet of Staple made the wrought iron chandelier and scrolled ironwork for a door, and another church member made the wrought iron flower-holders.

The blacksmith's grave is not far from that of the last Lord St Audries in the well-tended churchyard that preserves part of the ancient cross. His epitaph speaks eloquently:

'Francis Stone

1886 - 1965

Spent his lifetime in this Village

Blacksmith, Bellringer and Friend of all'.

This church has a set of old handbells used not only in church but for carol-singing in the village and elsewhere. A copy of a watercolour of the former old church hangs inside the door.

New houses have risen at Staple along the road to Bicknoller, but here one still finds the old sandstone cottages and former smithy as well as the mossy weathered buildings of Staple Farm. From this road one may strike off on the left towards the pretty hamlet of Weacombe under Weacombe Hill, past Weacombe House with its tiny lake. Foxgloves grow thick in Weacombe Combe (plate 8) and the hill-ponies shelter in Weacombe Glen that is threaded by a stream.

14. Combe Florey

'A very pretty place in very beautiful country', the Rev. Sydney Smith described this melodiously named village. Combe Florey conceals itself well away from the A358 in a striking red and green landscape similar to that surrounding its neighbour Bagborough, for here the sandstone of buildings is a specially vivid red and so is the soil of arable land, field-paths and tracks while the combe, or valley, is green with trees and watered by streams. The combe holds the main village street that crosses a stream by a tiny humped bridge.

'Florey' is derived from the name of de Fleuri, one of the Norman landowners of the place, who was followed by the families of de Meriet and Francis. All of them have memorials in the church of which the rose-red tower stands among beech trees on the crest of the combe. Several memorials are very striking, for instance the effigies of Sir John de Meriet and his two wives which recline in the north aisle. A knight of Edward III's time, he wears chain mail and rests his crossed legs on a lion. When these effigies were moved from under their original canopies fragments of oyster shells containing remains of the original pigments that painted them were discovered. A diminutive brass in the floor near

1. *Barford House, Enmore, a red-brick house dating from the eighteenth century, has been restored from near-ruin.*

2. *The Rogers Almshouse, Cannington, built as a Church House (c. 1500) and restored c. 1699 with money left by Henry Rogers.*

3. The tiny village of Aisholt, described by Coleridge as 'a deep romantic chasm . . . down a green hill'.

4. The wind-swept Holford Beeches stand beside the 'Great Road' on Longstone Hill.

5. The poet Coleridge lived in this cottage in Lime Street, Nether Stowey. It subsequently became an inn, but is now in the care of the National Trust.

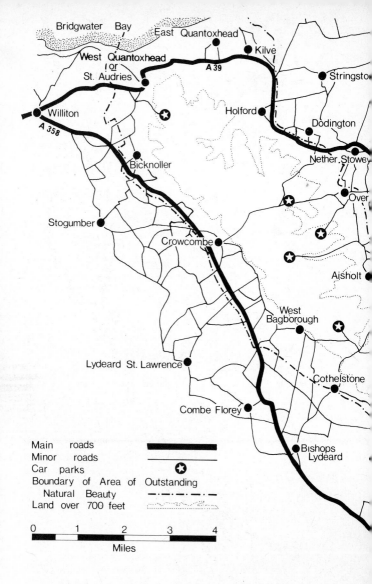

THE QUANTOCKS

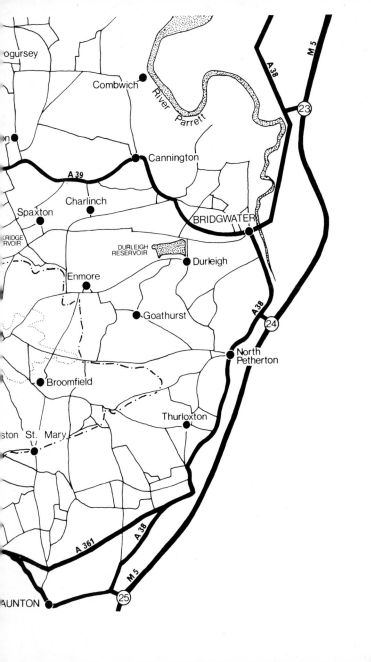

6. Kilve church and the ruined chantry, damaged when contra-band brandy-kegs hidden there by smugglers were set alight to thwart the excise officers.

7. St Mary's church, Court House and Court Farm by the village pond at East Quantoxhead.

8. The view down Weacombe Combe, near St Audries, towards Taunton Vale and the Brendon Hills.

9. The Church House at Crowcombe dates from 1515.

10. *Fyne Court, Broomfield, built in 1636, was partly destroyed by fire in 1898. The remaining portion is leased by the National Trust to the Somerset Trust for Nature Conservation.*

11. *Part of the Drove Track between Triscombe Stone and Crowcombe Combe Gate.*

the organ shows Florence Francis (1485) kneeling with her two children and wearing a butterfly head-dress. She lived for sixty-five years after this, the date of her husband's death. Most curious of all is the empty little heart-shrine in the north wall that once held the heart of Maud de Meriet who died, a nun, at the convent in Cannington. '*Le Quer Dame Maud de Meriet nonayne de Cannington*' spells the Lombardic lettering in Old French.

Opposite the church a stream runs along near a sandstone wall that hollows out over a mossy well. A steep grassy mound planted with trees and daffodils rises above the wall. It is called 'the monks' garden' and was perhaps the site of a Combe Florey chantry. In 1791 Collinson saw 'the remains of an old building used as a summer-house' here, perhaps an ancient dove-cote. Not far from the church stands the beautiful gatehouse (originally four-storeyed) of an Elizabethan manor-house built by the Francis family, using the local red stone. The manor-house has gone, the gatehouse is still used as a house. Over its archway we see the Francis coat-of-arms, and on its dripstone 'ER 1593'. An Elizabethan shilling was found over the keystone.

In the seventeenth century Thomas Francis built the dignified manor-house standing in the park today. The novelist Evelyn Waugh lived here during the last years of his life.

The Old Rectory above the church and village is a Queen Anne house surrounded by walled grounds. Here lived the wealthy, ebullient rector, Sydney Smith, who spent a lot of money on repairing it in the nineteenth century — hustling his Somerset workmen. He had sixty acres of land round it. He wrote admiringly of the lovely scenery at Combe Florey and ministered kindly to his flock in many ways, but as a townsman he found the country 'a kind of healthy grave'—'flowers, green turf, birds, are not worth an hour of rational conversation,' he wrote.

There is a very pretty house named The Old Manor House, charming old cottages and sandstone barns.

15. Lydeard St Lawrence

A pleasing route to this still remote village runs from Bishop's Lydeard across Ash Priors Common, cut by a stream, and through the village of Ash Priors. A maze of narrow red-tinged lanes rich in wild flowers, with ash-trees in high-banked hedges, connects with Lydeard St Lawrence while narrower redder field-paths lead to some of the old farms. The Southey family owned Holford Farm, the birthplace of the father of Robert Southey, the poet.

The village, lying in the lee of the Quantocks, consists of an up-and-down main street made up of interesting old houses, brown, red or cream-washed. The red sandstone church of St Lawrence the Martyr stands at the top of this street on a site where the finding of a flint arrow-head suggested the existence of an early settlement. The buttressed tower has eight pinnacles. The light, simple interior exerts considerable charm. In the fifteenth century the north aisle was added to the earlier nave and chancel. Its arcade has columns crowned by capitals beautifully carved with interesting motifs: a fox carrying a goose, heads and wings of angels, a foliage-trail, an interlace pattern reminiscent of Saxon design.

Twined branches are carved on some of the bench-ends. There is a squint with an iron bar, and a scratch dial near the priest's door.

16. West Bagborough

The road from Cothelstone to Bagborough has much to delight the eye. From the right-hand turn by the lodge marked Park End it runs past woodlands towards a line of beeches twisted fantastically by the wind and framing landscape stretching in an irregular coloured pattern towards the sea. Continuing straight on brings the traveller to Lydeard Hill car park which offers another splendid view and the starting-point of many Quantock walks including one of two miles to Triscombe Stone. But for Bagborough one bears left and downhill. This road too provides very beautiful Quantock views especially if you linger at a field-gate. From the gate opposite Tilbury Farm, where the view includes great trees and between them the ornamental lake of the Esdailes' vanished Cothelstone House, two unusual features catch the attention. One, a little way down the slope, is a folly in the form of a pretty half-ruined sandstone summer-house; the other, nearer the top hedge, is the crudely sculptured figure of a cloaked but nearly naked man (a huntsman or Jupiter?). He has a dog at his feet and surmounts a 'prospect seat'. These, with several other statues that have disappeared, were ornaments of an eighteenth-century park belonging to Tirhill House that stood here before the now demolished Cothelstone House. The landowner who placed them here was probably Thomas Slocombe whose memorial tablet is in Bishop's Lydeard church.

Bagborough has a lofty situation among sharply rising green pastures and fields with very red soil that make an authentic Quantock landscape of which this village, built of red sandstone once quarried here, is an integral part. Sandstone walls grow ivy and wallflower; red banks of lanes are thick with ferns.

Close to the church gate a stream trickles noisily through the little brick arch of a well hung with hart's tongue fern. The church path follows a most delightful course by the parkland of Bagborough House, the white slate-roofed Georgian house with Ionic capitals to its pillared portico, seen between firs and hollies on the right. In spring a drift of snowdrops spreads on the lawn under the trees. Wordsworth and his wife Mary stayed at this house, home of the Pophams, in 1841. The tracery of trees outlined itself against the silver-pink tower of the church (St Pancras). The high churchyard commands a superb view of the Vale of Taunton, hills, woods and farms and further to the Brendon Hills and distant Exmoor. In spring snowdrops, primroses and daffodils colour the grass among the many interesting mossy tombstones, one of which is inscribed to Eleanor Woodford (1695) in beautiful lettering, and another to William Chorley, Yeoman of this Parish, aged ninety-three, 1864. The church was restored in 1872 when much of it was in a poor state. There is however much to please and interest: the buttressed Perpendicular tower, the waggon-roofs (the typical Somerset type), with the old gilded bosses, the Tudor bench-ends carved with quaint faces and foliage, the tower screen carved by local people like the font cover on which the Passion emblems appear, the seventeenth-century memorial brass in the north aisle to Edward Kellet, Citizen of London, the two worn wooden figures of saints in the porch, the sun-dial dated 1648 over the porch.

One inn is called the Rising Sun, another, at Seven Ash, the Stag's Head, appropriately in this district where the Quantock Staghounds are kennelled and where this now controversial sport has been practised for centuries. Deer lie in Bagborough Wood.

At Chapel Cottages is Quantock Design pottery and gallery.

The tiny hamlet of Triscombe, composed of a few cottages and the Blue Ball Inn, lies off the A358 under Will's Neck, the highest point of the Quantock range. Will's Neck means Ridge of the Welshmen, meaning the Celtic tribe which fought the Saxons on this ridge and is said to have raised the cairn of stones. The Triscombe quarry has very regrettably eaten away a great portion of the hillside. Triscombe may be reached on foot by a rough hill-track descending from Triscombe Stone near Quantock Farm.

17. Bishop's Lydeard

King Alfred gave land in this locality to Asser, Bishop of Sherborne. No doubt a Saxon church stood here then, probably where the present church stands in the heart of the village. The church tower is the chief glory of the place. It was the first of the noble towers of west Somerset to be built.

Apart from the new estates, for this is a growing place, the whole village is built of deep red sandstone, much of it from its own quarries such as Lydeard Quarry near the church. Church, the greater houses, farmhouses, cottages, barns, garden and churchyard walls that grow pink valerian and wallflowers are of the same warm rosy colour. The tower glows red in sunset light. A few old cottages are colour-washed yellow or cream so that the continuous line of Mount Street, Church Street and West Street has been described as 'one long pink-and-yellow street'.

The red sandstone almshouses are one of the oldest features of High Street, built in 1616 by Richard Grobham in memory of his parents, his father Nicholas being further commemorated by a brass in the church that depicts a child blowing bubbles. Other fine old buildings, as well as modern builders' and engineers' premises that replace some of the craftsmen's workshops seen twenty years ago, are tucked away down 'drangs' and side-alleys. Down Mill Lane, past a lovely thatched house where the miller used to live, one follows a noisy stream to the calm leat and disused 'overshot' wheel of Darby's Mill that has belonged to several generations of a family and is still in use for agricultural purposes. It is a big cream-washed stone building with a portico over the house door and a millstone resting against its garden wall. Old Vicarage Lane leads to a garden full of trees and the old sandstone rectory. The former blacksmith's shop hides away near the antique shop. Notable, too, are the inns with their pretty names, the Gardeners' Arms, the Bird in Hand, the picturesque Bell near the church, and the Lethbridge Arms named after the family that owned Sandhill Park, a great house made into a hospital.

The lovely pinnacled church tower was built in 1470, built without interruption as its buttresses flowing into the pinnacles seem to indicate. As at Kingston the tracery of the belfry windows is lace-like. All its dressings are of golden Ham freestone. Sir John Stawell of Cothelstone stored weapons in this tower during the Civil War when a field called Standards is supposed to have acquired its name. Several wartime origins have been attributed to the name of Conquest Farm.

The chief adornment of this church is its superb woodwork, not least the graceful fan-vaulted fifteenth-century screen carved with the words of the Creed in Latin. Tudor wood-carvers (and there is no support for the theory that they were Flemish and not Somerset craftsmen) made the splendid and interesting bench-ends that display a post-mill with the miller on his horse, Jack-in-the-Green, the Five Wounds, the Passion emblems, a hunted stag and the Pelican in Piety, crest of Richard Fox, Bishop of Bath and Wells in

1492. The Jacobean pulpit too is finely carved. A local craftsman made the oak screen of the vestry in the tower, where a window contains beautiful fragments of stained glass found during the restoration of 1850. They illustrate the sacrament of baptism and made part of a window that illustrated the seven sacraments.

The south door has an iron handle and lock several centuries old, with a beam-bolt. Two ancient crosses stand in the church-yard: one is a Calvary (fourteenth-century) sculptured with weather-worn figures that include St John the Baptist, the other a market-cross from the village with Virgin and Child sculptured in one of its niches.

Standing near the market-cross one obtains a good view of eighteenth-century Lydeard House which is built of sandstone with freestone ornamentation including an elegant balustrade to its garden walls. Its gatehouse with clock and lantern is of earlier date.

---

18. Cothelstone

A manor-house, a church dedicated to St Thomas of Canterbury (Becket), scattered farms and a handful of cottages compose this little village set in lovely surroundings. The road from Bishop's Lydeard passes Cothelstone Manor before winding up Cothelstone Hill between red earth-banks held together by the exposed ser-pentine roots of grey beeches. At the top, right, it leads to a hill-top that was once a beacon-site and commands a far-flung land-scape containing parts of several counties. This hill-top is generally called Cothelstone Beacon. Two of its features are a group of wind-torn, scarred beeches called Cothelstone Clump which seem to be nearing their end (a new grove of young beeches has been planted near them and enclosed for protection)and the foundations of a ruined folly-tower, built about 1770 by Lady Hillsborough (born Stawell). Romantic people call it 'a hunting-tower'. Photographs taken about forty years ago show the round tower, badly damaged by gales and on the point of collapse. In 1973 the Somerset County Council bought 225 acres of Cothelstone Hill to preserve it for public enjoyment. Paradise, Badger's Copse and Much Care Wood (along the left-hand road, near Lydeard Hill car park) are a few of the picturesque names given to the woodlands of oak and beech in this locality. Lately considerable felling has taken place.

The Elizabethan manor-house of rosy sandstone with baluster-shaped mullions and a stone tablet displaying the Stawell coat-of-arms over its doorway was reduced to partial ruin in the Civil War.

Sir John Stawell, its Royalist defender, returned there to die after years in prison. His memorial is in the church.

In 1685 another Sir John, though equally Royalist, refused to receive Judge Jeffreys. In consequence two Somerset gentlemen involved in the Monmouth Rebellion were hanged on the gateposts. Mr Edward J. Esdaile skilfully restored the ruined portion of the house in 1855. The untouched Elizabethan gatehouse stands at the head of the avenue entered from the outer gateway. (This is the way to the church. The manor-house may be glimpsed from it, not visited.) The gatehouse is adorned by tripartite windows with shell-niches of yellow Ham stone that also makes the mullions. A Bishop's Lydeard craftsman replaced the diamond panes broken in the Second World War. Left, a path leads past very old red cottages to the tucked-away church, so appealing in its smallness and simplicity. Three of its fifteenth-century windows display six English saints: Dunstan, Cuthbert, Aldhelm, Richard of Chichester, Thomas of Hereford, Thomas of Canterbury. The Stawell chapel contains fine alabaster effigies: Sir John, and his wife, builder of the manor-house who raised one thousand men to fight the Spaniards, and the medieval knight Sir Matthew Stawell with his wife, Eleanor de Merton, whose feet rest on little squirrels. Bench-ends offer a wealth of Tudor carving — berries, roses, foliage and birds.

In the churchyard a tombstone with a dove is inscribed 'In sweet memory of Ianthe, daughter of the poet Shelley'. She married Edward Jeffries Esdaile whose father had built in 1818 a dignified mansion called Cothelstone House, situated in the park where its ornamental lake remains. This house, home of Ianthe and subsequent Esdailes, was demolished in recent years.

Just inside a field a little way up the hill a small stream runs to feed St Agnes' Well — an old holy well. Greenery hides the ruined well-house.

19. Kingston St Mary

In spite of recent tree-felling the approach to Kingston down steeply undulating Buncombe Hill from The Pines Garage crossroads is still sylvan and accompanied all the way by a stream that waters the lower slopes of steeply pitched fields and in its time has served mills and tanyards in the village, part of which is named Mill Cross. Such farm-names as Yarford, Tarr and Ivyton have the authentic Somerset ring. The farm-name Loads indicates the lode of copper that was worked at one time. The famous cider apple or black apple called Kingston Black and extensively cultivated in Kingston orchards some years ago is supposed to owe its flavour to the copper in the soil.

Some of the old family names are pinned on to properties: the cottages with dormer windows (now one house) near the Swan Inn were called Bobbetts, and a gabled house in the middle of Kingston has Winpenny Farm on its gate. The name Camplin is attached to another house — two Camplins were Kingston vicars.

Sturdy old barns and stables, built of sandstone that has weathered to many gradations of red, and roofed with russet tiles overrun by lichen, contribute much to the composition of this beautiful village. Some of them are, of course, now transformed into houses and replaced by Dutch barns. An old barn at Church Farm by the churchyard has pigeon-holes in one wall. Tiles, thatch, plaster, pink and white wash, and predominantly the red sandstone from the parish's own quarries provide great variety, yet harmony, in the materials, styles and methods used by the makers of this place. And the church is its crown, literally and figuratively. It is set high, adjacent to pastures, half-ringed by hills, enclosed by a walled churchyard whose aged yews shade several beautiful eighteenth-century tombs patterned with green moss and silver lichen. Its exquisite tower, 'the perfected model' of a group of noble towers — as it was called by A. K. Wickham in *Churches of Somerset* — dominates the surrounding scene by reason of its height, grace, simplicity of line and richness of ornament which includes pierced battlements, a tier of quatrefoils, buttresses, pinnacles and lacelike tracery to its windows. Like the chancel and the south porch with its lovely fan-vaulting it was built in the fifteenth century; nave and aisles are older. Pinnacles and other ornaments are of yellow Ham stone. The main stonework of the church is red sandstone weathered and lichen-stained to a dusty pink. The exterior walls show pieces of ragstone and Ham stone, even a lump of azurite (its green colour due to copper) and pieces of slate mingled with the sandstone. They witness to the number of quarries once worked in the parish. A walk round the outside of this church reveals many little features of beauty or quaintness like the seventeenth-century tablet topped by a skull near the priest's door, a bearded face sculptured inside a quatrefoil, the angels holding shields carved in the bell-openings. None could miss the grotesque 'hunky-punks' carved sprawling on the tower-sides.

Space is lacking to describe the interior adequately, but luckily there is a most excellent guide to this church by H. F. Ellis — if only every Quantock church had one as good! A wealth of local craftsmanship helped to adorn this church. The superb brass chandelier or 'Branch' inscribed *'Thos Bayley fecit 1773'* is one of this Bridgwater craftsman's best. Thomas Kingston, a local man, carved the pulpit in 1743. A modern craftsman made the cabinet holding a black-letter Bible of the early seventeenth century. Tudor wood-carvers decorated the bench-ends with twined flowers, hands holding a rosary, oxen with their yokes, and significantly, a weaver's shuttle, a sign of the trade that helped pay for such towers and churches.

The huge altar-tomb, decorated with twenty-two painted shields, that stands in the Hestercombe chapel at the east end of the south aisle is traditionally linked with John de la Warre who lived at the house called Hestercombe after fighting at Poitiers and capturing the French king, John, whose sword he brought home. Again according to tradition, the shelf on an adjacent pillar was the sword's resting place. Certainly Hestercombe retained a great sword, inscribed with the cross and the sacred monogram IHS and on the reverse side, with *'En gladium Johnannis Galliae R'*, until 1872 when the Warre family sold the house. Glass in the south window painted with the arms of Warres and families connected to them was brought from the chapel at Hestercombe. The little glass panel of German glass (seventeenth-century) in the east window has charming detail that needs close scrutiny. At the west end of the aisle beautifully lettered memorial brasses to Dykes, Aclands and Herberts are on the walls of the Tetton House pew.

Hestercombe House had in its grounds a quarry that produced the red sandstone used in building Taunton church-towers. The greater part of this house, now in the hands of the County Fire Service, was rebuilt in 1872. Its gardens were designed and planted by Gertrude Jekyll and are now being restored to her original schemes. There is a charming orangery designed by Sir Edwin Lutyens.

The most beautiful house in Kingston is the manor-house, seen over the churchyard wall across a field. Robert Knight built it in 1560. Thomas Knight who had 'Thomas and Mary Knight 1702' carved on it made lavish alterations and added sash windows.

20. Broomfield

Broom and gorse flower abundantly on the remaining commons inside this hill-top parish and in summer purple foxgloves stand high in the bracken. There are spinneys of ash-trees, primroses in well-watered valleys and — revealed by recent fellings — lakes of bluebells in the woods of Buncombe, alongside the road to Kingston St Mary and one of the most beautiful Quantock places. From the same crossroads (near The Pines Garage) another road leads to Broomfield. It dominates a fine Quantock landscape of up-and-down green and red fields interspersed with oaks and elms and stretching seawards. Further on there are remnants of a famous avenue of ancient beeches, recently cut down, that screened the grounds of Fyne Court.

Part of this house (plate 10), built in 1636 and damaged by fire in 1898, remains. The property, given to the National Trust in 1972, is leased to the Somerset Trust for Nature Conservation. Here lived Andrew Crosse, the wealthy Quantock squire famous as 'the thunder-and-lightning man' for his pioneer experiments with electricity. One of the 'masts' he used still remains in one of the trees. Scientific societies respected him and Humphry Davy came to visit him and his laboratory. Crosse passionately loved his native heath, its flowers and wild creatures, and walked miles in the Quantocks with his young second wife Cornelia, writer and journalist, who erected his modestly inscribed monument in the churchyard: 'He was humble towards God and kind to his fellow-creatures.'

The riven thousand-year old yew mentioned in Crosse's writings survives in the churchyard. A table he used in the five-windowed Music Room that served as his laboratory and which, like the library, has now been beautifully restored and is used for concerts, stands in the beautiful little church (All Saints) of which notable features are an early fourteenth-century chancel, an arcade of 1535, waggon roof, and pier-capitals delicately sculptured with leaves. It is celebrated for the rich yet refined carving of its six-teenth-century bench-ends. The carver cut his name, Simon Werman.

An unusual brass on the tower floor depicts a Broomfield priest, Richard Silverman (1443), vested for mass and bearing the chalice. It was found under the boards.

Ruborough Camp on Broomfield Hill rises behind Rockhouse Farm and is approached by a rough red path. It can be reached via the lane near the Travellers' Rest on the Enmore-Taunton road (turn left at the corner). This triangular Iron Age fort covering seventeen acres, protected by earthworks and a deep fosse, is extremely impressive and has created legend. The area inside the ramparts, overgrown by wild sage, is called the Moneyfield because a demon-guarded castle full of gold, entered by an iron door, is believed to lie beneath. A clergyman called Dr Farrer and his manservant actually dug here on a night of full moon two hundred years ago, exposed the iron door and narrowly escaped being dragged underground by shrieking demons. There are springs that ensured a water-supply to defenders.

In Holwell Combe near Tudballs Farm a cave in the hillside, called Holwell Cavern, is hung with stalactites and has walls glittering with crystals formed by the action of water impregnated by limestone. So say people who have visited it, including Andrew Crosse who used its water in experiments, but breakage of stalagmites by visitors brought about its closure.

21. Crowcombe

From the A39, between Stowey and Holford, the road to Crowcombe is the winding Coach Road which climbs past Five Lords Combe on the left, where charcoal-burners worked, and Danesborough. Nearby is the site of Walford's Gibbet, where Walford, a charcoal-burner, was hanged. He created a legend. At the top it turns left to run along moorland and near Quantock Farm plunges down a combe to the valley enclosing the village just off the A358. At the top of the combe there is a splendid view of Fire Beacon Hill and Will's Neck but wooded banks enclose the combe-road where until a few years ago their over-arching beeches made a green tunnel, a place for bluebells and many birds. A right-hand turn at the bottom leads to the church, Crowcombe Court and the Church House with adjoining cattle-pound, an arresting group. (There is a car park behind the Church House.) This almost unique building is one of the oldest in the Quantocks. Surviving church houses are extremely rare; the only other in Somerset is at Chew Magna. The Crowcombe building was rescued from semi-ruin in the present century, having served as a village school from 1661 to 1871. At one time the lower storey made an almshouse; an outside flight of hollowed steps leads to the upper floor. Its original use was the holding of church-ales and village festivities so that the present use as village hall is appropriate. It existed from 1515 (plate 9).

Crowcombe Court, a mansion of mellowed brick and yellow Ham stone, linked by a pavilion to an array of handsome stable buildings, was built by 1725, largely to the design of Nathaniel Ireson of Wincanton, for young Thomas Carew who planted the woods about it. This house, accounted one of the finest in Somerset, has some magnificent interior features. A few years ago it stood unoccupied, considerably damaged by fire, but recently much restoration has been carried out.

The Perpendicular church (the Holy Ghost) is a treasure. Grotesque heads and animals are carved below its battlements. The south porch with its lovely fan-vaulting has a parvise above. The later south aisle arcade has arches of pink sandstone. The Perpendicular font of yellow stone is sculptured with an uncommon pattern of convolvulus and with figures of St Anne reading to the Virgin, a knight at prayer, a bishop raising his hand in blessing. The Carews' chapel — their arms are painted above the panelling — was built in 1655.

This church is celebrated for the superb Tudor carvings on its bench-ends, one of which bears the date 1534. Mermen, dragons, monsters, Jack-in-the-Green, sprays of greenery, naked men fighting — their variety of motif, more pagan than Christian, and the robust exuberance of their execution, make them as fascinating to study each time a visitor returns. The high altar was carved by a skilled modern Crowcombe craftsman.

The graceful Perpendicular churchyard cross is sculptured with the almost obliterated figures of a bishop and a prioress. An equally graceful market-cross with steps (Crowcombe used to be a little borough with a market as early as 1226) stands in the village where many cottages survive whose picturesque charms have set them on calendars and watercolour sketches. Some retain thatched roofs that one sometimes sees being renewed by a skilled Quantock thatcher. The rectory close to the churchyard is an Elizabethan house.

The ruins of Cardinal Beaufort's Chapel (fifteenth-century) hide in the woods behind Crowcombe Court, set there by Mr Carew who brought them from Halsway Manor. There is a tradition that Cardinal Beaufort, who tried Joan of Arc, owned a house at Halsway, a mile north-west of Crowcombe (off the A358). The present Halsway Manor, a gabled house of red sandstone, has considerable charm but is not as Tudor as it looks, having undergone much rebuilding. A boss on its hall roof is carved with a portcullis, the Beaufort badge. This house, now in the hands of the Halsway Manor Society, is a centre for folk dance. Various conferences and courses are held there and, during the Minehead Arts Festival, recitals and first-class chamber concerts.

22. Stogumber

A very beautiful village dominated by a splendid church and lying between the Quantocks and the Brendons, Stogumber has been chosen for special conservation. Almost every house on the banks of the steep street evokes admiration, for instance the house made from six old almshouses where originally six poor widows received one shilling each weekly from the owner of Combe Sydenham, and the house called Seven Crosses with its medieval doorways that have ornamental ironwork and handrails to their flights of steps. The wrought iron ring was made, like the parish room gates, by the former smith at the hamlet of Vellow, where potter David Winkley makes hand-thrown vitreous ovenproof stoneware in the old forge. The road to Vellow brings you to old buttressed cottages and at a place of many streams where there was a holy well, to cottages that incorporate a former chantry. In a field of one Stogumber farm there is a spring called Harry Hill's Well. At one time its water was used in brewing the celebrated Stogumber ale.

Opposite the church and joining the White Horse Inn an eighteenth-century reading room stands on a corner, a curving flight of steps with iron handrail leading to its door. A gaping stone dragon sprawls across one side of the red fourteenth-century church tower. The red sandstone arcade of the south aisle is equally old. The north aisle of greyer sandstone was traditionally built by Cardinal Beaufort whose badge, a portcullis, adorns a boss in the north chapel. The aisle pillars have capitals sculptured with leaves, emblems of the Passion, the Five Wounds and the branch-entwined face of Jack-in-the-Green. The door to the rood-loft is adorned with very lovely medieval ironwork and fluted ring-handle in wrought iron.

The fine brass chandelier (rediscovered in a lumber room) was made by Thomas Bayley of Bridgwater (1770). The fifteenth-century stone pulpit is an unusual feature. There are roundels of Flemish glass in the south aisle window, and in a recess in the north aisle a brass to Margery Wyndham (1585), interestingly depicted wearing a French hood and pleated skirt.

Sydenhams of Combe Sydenham built the south chapel which is dominated by the tomb of 'Sir Gorge Sidnum' as it was spelt by the rustic carver of the effigies of Sir George, his two wives and three babies, dated 1596. Its canopy is of richer, more skilled workmanship.

Combe Sydenham lies near Monksilver and was the subject of Richard Jefferies's essay 'A Manor-House in Red Deer Land'. It is a red stone manor-house with a tower and very old farm buildings in front of it. Tradition holds that Elizabeth Sydenham, betrothed to Drake far away on a voyage, left this house to marry another man in Stogumber church but changed her mind en route when a cannon-ball, fired across the world, dropped at her feet as a sign of Drake's anger. She did indeed marry Drake. 'Drake's cannon-ball', a meteorite, remains at Combe Sydenham where Richard Jefferies saw it. The house now opens to the public.

The famous old Heddon Oak (recently felled) stood beside the road to Crowcombe. Three rebels of the Monmouth Rebellion were hanged on it.

Several notable craftsmen live in Stogumber. One of them carved the high altar in the church.

23. Bicknoller

New building has not enhanced the beauty of this place. Nevertheless it remains one of the most beautiful Quantock villages in a situation second to none. Thorncombe Hill, Bicknoller Hill, Halsway Hill and Weacombe Hill draw generous curves around it. In autumn their larches, ashes, beeches, birches, and bracken hang a tawny backcloth that makes perfect camouflage for red deer in their combes. At night deer often come down Long Combe, Paradise Combe and Halsway Combe to plunder orchards and fields. As at Holford the rutting stag's belling can be heard in November.

A huge barrow crowns Thorncombe Hill. On the steep side (not the top) of Bicknoller Hill is sited the circular Iron Age Camp of Trendle Ring. There are old quarries nearby that provided red sandstone for building Bicknoller and other villages.

The nature-writer Richard Jefferies came here in summer and was enchanted. Today he would miss most of the oakwoods, some of the meadows, the mill, and the little yew sown by a bird and growing on the church tower. Many can still remember the latter; tower and yew-tree are carved on one of four modern bench-ends (1932) in the church. However Jefferies would still find the split black yew propped up in the churchyard and the cross silvered by lichens. Jefferies described Bicknoller in *Summer in Somerset*, illustrated by his friend J. W. North who lodged with him at a farmhouse, now Woolston Grange. Frederick Walker painted his famous picture 'The Plough' at Woolston.

The stonework of the church (St George) is similarly silvered. Most of the building, once a chapelry of Stogumber, is early fifteenth-century work. The tower, with its grotesque winged beasts, the porch and north aisle were built a century later. The porch has a stone stairway leading to a parvise. Windows are ancient, but some have been moved, some blocked and uncovered, some mutilated then well restored. Note the north Perpendicular window (1450) with three cinquefoil lights in the chancel, and also the tracery of two on its south side (1530); in the north aisle, west wall, the oldest (1430) and its east window (1500); in the chancel the north window in which fragments of old stained glass have been sympathetically assembled. Some of the modern glass too is pleasing, notably the window in the south side of the chancel, by Martin Travers (1936), depicting a 'medieval' Virgin in blue and red, with Child.

The fan-vaulted screen is supposedly one of seven carved c. 1500 by a group of craftsmen centred at Dunster. Early Tudor carvings, foliate and floral, grace the oldest bench-ends. The capitals of columns are sculptured with wreaths of foliage, instruments of the Passion, the Five Wounds, and the figure of Gluttony.

A tablet on a bench near the font is inscribed 'William Temple, Archbishop [of York], worshipped here on holiday 1933-1944'.

The village is very pretty, a diversity of old houses and cottages with thatch, cream or yellow plaster, brown tiles, brickwork, red sandstone walls, making a harmonious composition. One house is haunted by a lady who plays a spinet.

24. Williton

This small town on the river Willett is a good centre for the Quantocks and the sea as the roads to Taunton, Bridgwater and Minehead meet here. For all its new development it retains its essentially west Somerset houses with white walls and thatch. Part of the manor-house, Orchard Wyndham, dates from 1500. Wyndhams ardently supported the Royalist cause in the Civil War.

Richard Fitz Urse (died 1168) had a house and lands here; his son, Reginald, was one of Becket's four murderers, and tradition maintains that another son, in expiation, built a chapel that developed into the present little church of St Peter of which the walls contain some stones from an older building.

Close to the road to Watchet there lies a field gruesomely named Battlegore. Mounds in the centre are prehistoric barrows and are not connected with Danes despite local legends, although the field-name may spring from a fight with Danish raiders.

In Blackdown Wood (privately owned) the monument locally known as Mother Shipton's Tomb is really a nineteenth-century copy of a memorial stone in Cumberland to a little Roman girl called Julia Martima. It is sculptured with her head and a wreath.

25. Watchet

With its numerous new bungalows, souvenir shops and rebuilt harbour Watchet is now a very different place from the little port whence Coleridge's Ancient Mariner supposedly set sail. However, it is still a place of considerable character, possessing a number of old houses and inns and an interesting Baptist chapel (1824). The paper mills and other enterprises gave renewed life to the port; Dutch, Russian and Scandinavian boats often lie in the harbour. Visitors can fish from the two piers.

The chief glory is the splendid Perpendicular church of St Decuman with its lofty towers. It stands apart in fields. This church merits detailed description and a prolonged visit. Among its Wyndham brasses is one to Florence Wyndham who, in about 1560, was roused from presumed death by the sexton's cutting her finger to steal her rings, so that she returned, shrouded, from the vault to the Wyndham home at Kentisford, now an old farmhouse. The packhorse bridge is called Kentisford Bridge. West of the church there is St Decuman's Well where this Celtic evangelist washed his head which had been cut off by his enemies, and replaced it — he lived on, leading an active life!

The Danes ravaged Watchet several times.

The town may owe its name, meaning 'blue', to its blue lias cliffs where Defoe found caves 'lined with alabaster', which was much used for monuments.

Postscript

Amongst other places in the Quantocks area are the following, of which Stogursey, Dodington and North Petherton should not be missed:

Stogursey on the seaward side of the A39, with its magnificent Norman priory church, priory, dovecote, remains of the castle and mill almshouses. It is reached via the Hinkley Point road from Cannington, and has been named for conservation. Restoration has started on the castle and mill sites.

Dodington, a little village also on the seaward side with very red fields, old copper-mine installations, tiny sandstone church and Elizabethan Dodington Hall. Permission is granted to visit the hall of this house which retains its minstrels' gallery. The parish contains the attractive house called the Castle of Comfort (on A39) formerly an inn of that name and mentioned in Dorothy Wordsworth's *Journal*. Travelling westwards, turn right for Dodington after leaving Nether Stowey.

North Petherton, on A38, three miles from Bridgwater. The church of this very large expanding village possesses one of the noblest towers in Somerset, nearly 110 feet high. The Alfred Jewel was found in low marshy country in this parish. The church has a replica; the original is in the Ashmolean Museum, Oxford. The Kingscliff valley is very beautiful and the country beyond it well worth exploring (turn off opposite the church).

Fiddington. Although the cottage of the former smithy, at the corner where the Fiddington lane runs off the A39, resembles an illustration to a fairy-tale there is an ancient devil-legend attached to it. Holly-trees abound in the lanes. The church (St Martin) is mostly Victorian but has a Perpendicular tower. In the churchyard there are the remains of an old cross. The potter John Harlow makes very attractive domestic stoneware in his workshop in a former farmhouse where the barn has become a showroom.

Lilstock, reached by lane and fieldpath, is a tiny Somerset harbour built early in the nineteenth century by Sir Peregrine Acland of Fairfield, Stogursey. Remains of the harbour are still visible; so are the ruined lime-kilns, one of its chief sources of trade, close to the jagged blue-grey-yellow cliffs that are crumbling and perilous. Here Sir Peregrine built a kind of chalet for his young invalid daughter and a turfed promenade so that she might enjoy carriage drives as well as sea air. She recovered her health. Part of these installations remains.

In a wildly overgrown churchyard at the side of a quiet lane those who search will find the remains of the medieval chapel of St Andrew, of which the chancel was enlarged in the nineteenth century to make a church. The building now lies deserted, left to the ravages of weather and vandals. On its walls there are memorial tablets to Pophams and Luttrells. The Norman font, green with algae, should be preserved in another church.

Among the graves outside there is the grave of Sarah Perrett, a Lilstock girl who became a servant at Windsor Castle and whom Queen Victoria made personal servant to the young Princess Alexandra, even sending her to Denmark to travel with the princess to England.

Suggested walks

The hills are criss-crossed with paths, which lead down into a beautiful combe or up on to the crest of another hill.

1. The Ridgeway or Pack Way, the spine road

A good eleven miles, but easy going. A walker who leaves his car at Lydeard Hill car park near West Bagborough (a good starting point) will need to be met at Staple car park at the other end of the ridge.) The Minehead-Bridgwater bus no. 215 serves the non-motorist at the Staple end (picked up on the A39). Bus no. 218 connects Taunton with Williton and Minehead, Crowcombe lies just off the route.

The section from Lydeard Hill to Triscombe Stone (Triscombe Stone is a wishing stone. Sit on it and wish!) is locally called the Alfred Road; the section from Triscombe Stone to Crowcombe

Park Gate is known as the Drove Road and runs between ancient beeches.

On the left, starting from Lydeard Hill, there are fine views of the Brendons and a glimpse of Exmoor, and a closer one of the swelling Quantock slopes of Will's Neck, Crowcombe Fire Beacon, Hurley Beacon and others. On the right one sees the Bristol Channel, the island Holms, the Welsh coast. The path runs through bracken, gorse-bushes, whortleberry-bushes, rough grass where sheep graze. Prehistoric burial mounds are visible. This road can be reached from Crowcombe (car park behind the Church House) by a climb up the Crowcombe Combe road; if by car, there is a car park at Dead Woman's Ditch on the hilltop. *The laying of a hard surface for motor traffic on any part of the Ridgeway is vigorously opposed by all lovers of the hills.*

2. Walks from Holford

Holford is served by bus 215. Cars are left at the lay-by at the foot of Woodlands Hill alongside A39, a lane near the lay-by leading to the village.

a: Up Butterfly (Tannery) Combe, past Combe House and the mill wheel, into a big grassy glade where the combe opens out and where children paddle in the stream, past the pool, under overhanging oaks and beeches, over stepping-stones to trace the source of the brook which is a little spring called Lady's Fountain in the shadow of Danesborough (Dowsborough) on the left.

b: Up Dog Pound Lane near Alfoxton. Follow the old Great Road under the Holford beeches (view of the sea and Kilve). On Longstone Hill it is moorland country; the fallen stone is hidden. Not far from Bicknoller Post the road joins the Packway and runs to Staple (St Audries),

or at Bicknoller Post one may take the zigzag path leading back to Sheppard's Combe and Holford.

c: Cross the Bowling Green to Hodder's Combe, close to Willoughby Cleeve, the lovely woods given to the National Trust by Mr and Mrs Falk. These are fine trees (under preservation order). Parts of the terrain are boggy. In Sheppard's Combe there are foxgloves, spindle-trees, hawthorns. On top it is moorland. Walk to Bicknoller Post, then to the triangulation survey stone on Beacon Hill for wide views.

3. The Greenway Path

Alongside Smith's Combe, off A39, in the parish of East Quantoxhead (car park in quarry nearby) the Greenway Path climbs to join the Great Road. From Beacon Hill walk past a deer

gate to West Hill then walk down to Perry on the A39. This
revolving, circular iron gate, locally known as Funny Gate, was
made by a Stogursey smith.

4. To Bicknoller Post

Leaving the car at Staple, walk to Bicknoller Post which is a
centre for many paths leading to Weacombe and other combes
and hills.

The same description applies to Halsey Post near the other end
of the range.

5. Danesborough

From the Coach Road (Crowcombe road off A39) turn right
near the head of Five Lords Combe and use the track called
Danesborough Ditch. Take one of the narrow paths through
scrub-oak to the summit camp (you may see deer in the scrub)
or take lower paths over slopes of Danesborough (Dowsborough)
for Holford.

6. The Quantock Trail

Follow the Over Stowey road off A39. Go straight ahead at
Marshmills, then fork left to Adscombe. The 2½-mile Trail starts
at Seven Wells Bridge and takes you through a Quantock forest
laid down in 1922. At the hut you may buy a good guide. There are
eight stopping-places. At Ramscombe there is a picnic area and
car park. Deer tracks, remains of charcoal-burning and squirrels'
dreys may be observed as well as trees of great variety. Seven Wells
Bridge is at the junction of Ramscombe and Quantock Combe.
There is an old holy well (St David's) in Quantock Combe.

7. Lydeard Hill and Bagborough

From Lydeard Hill car park, past the gate, take the path on the
left and walk down to Bagborough village. Take the path through
the beautiful churchyard, follow a footpath bearing left into a
field whence a path leads to a lane serving Rock Farm and
Smokeham Farm. A left-hand turn leads to Triscombe (woodland
on one side); a right-hand turn leads back to Lydeard Hill.

8. From Kilve

There is a car park in Kilve village. Follow Pardlestone Lane up
Pardlestone Hill, go along the top of Alfoxton Park to Holford
Beeches and down Dog Pound Lane to the Bowling Green. Bear
left, fork left round Holford Glen. A field-gate near the Plough
Inn leads to a footpath over fields to join Hunt's Lane which joins
A39 not far from Kilve village.

9. Cockercombe and Keeper's Combe

Walk the pretty country road from Quantock Lodge School

which is on the Marshmills-Plainsfield route and explore beautiful Cockercombe and Keeper's Combe.

Bibliography

The Alfoxden Journal; Dorothy Wordsworth.

Churches of Somerset; A. K. Wickham; David & Charles.

Coleridge and Wordsworth in Somerset; Berta Lawrence; David & Charles.

The Land of Quantock; Rev. W. Greswell; Taunton, 1903.

Men and Mining in the Quantocks; John Hamilton and J. F. Lawrence; Town & Country Press.

Portrait of the Quantocks; Vincent Waite; Robert Hale.

Quantock Country; Berta Lawrence; Westaway Books.

The Quantock Hills; Beatrice Cresswell; John Whitby & Son.

Quantock Life and Rambles; Rev. E. H. Smith; Wessex Press.

Somerset (South and West); Nikolaus Pevsner; Penguin.

Roads for motorists

1. The A39: Bridgwater-Cannington-Nether Stowey-Holford-Kilve-St Audries-Williton-Minehead.

2. The A358: Taunton-Bishop's Lydeard-Crowcombe-Bicknoller-Williton.

3. From Nether Stowey up Castle Hill to Bincombe Green; climb to the top, turn left, then turn right and downward to Crowcombe (narrow and very steep).

4. From the A39 the Crowcombe Road (signposted) turns left between Nether Stowey and Holford. Climb to the top and join no. 3 at Dead Woman's Ditch. The road through Crowcombe joins A358.

5. The Bridgwater-Enmore road to the Travellers' Rest and The Pines Garage, where a signpost indicates four possible routes:

a. The road to Broomfield

b. The road down to Kingston St Mary.

c. The road to Park End, where turn left to Cothelstone and Bishop's Lydeard.

d. Also to Park End, then right (a narrow road) to West Bagborough.

It is absolutely essential that cars are not driven on the hills (off the roads) and that as far as possible the official car parks are used (Dead Woman's Ditch, Lydeard Hill, near Triscombe Stone, the Quantock Trail, and Staple).

Index

Printed by C. I. Thomas & Sons (Haverfordwest) Ltd., Press Buildings, Merlin's Bridge, Haverfordwest, Pembrokeshire.